I0797560

¡Tu increíble cuerpo! / Your Amazing Body!

TUS OÍDOS
YOUR EARS

Nancy Greenwood
Traducido por / Translated by Esther Ortiz

Please visit our website, www.garethstevens.com. For a free color catalog of all our high-quality books, call toll free 1-800-542-2595 or fax 1-877-542-2596.

Library of Congress Cataloging-in-Publication Data

Names: Greenwood, Nancy, author.
Title: Your ears = Tus oídos / Nancy Greenwood.
Description: New York : Gareth Stevens Publishing, [2019] | Series: Your amazing body! = ¡Tu increíble cuerpo! | Includes index.
Identifiers: LCCN 2017044173| ISBN 9781538227893 (library bound)
Subjects: LCSH: Ear–Juvenile literature. | Hearing–Juvenile literature.
Classification: LCC QP462.2 .G745 2019 | DDC 612.8/5–dc23
LC record available at https://lccn.loc.gov/2017044173

Published in 2019 by
Gareth Stevens Publishing
111 East 14th Street, Suite 349
New York, NY 10003

Translator: Esther Ortiz
Editorial Director, Spanish: Nathalie Beullens-Maoui
Editor, English: Kate Mikoley
Designer: Bethany Perl

Photo credits: Cover, pp. 1 (boy), 19 AJP/Shutterstock.com; p. 1 (gym) dotshock/Shutterstock.com; p. 5 (boy) Ilya Andriyanov/Shutterstock.com; p. 5 (playground) Marco Saroldi/Shutterstock.com; p. 7 (girl) Kasefoto/Shutterstock.com; p. 7 (park) Werayuth Tes/Shutterstock.com; p. 9 Tom Wang/Shutterstock.com; p. 11 Vladimir Gjorgiev/Shutterstock.com; pp. 13, 24 ilikestudio/Shutterstock.com; pp. 15, 24 (girl) espies/Shutterstock.com; pp. 15, 24 (bedroom) Artazum/Shutterstock.com; pp. 17, 24 didesign021/Shutterstock.com; p. 21 Eric Isselee/Shutterstock.com; p. 23 wavebreakmedia/Shutterstock.com.

Printed in the United States of America

CPSIA compliance information: Batch #CS18GS: For further information contact Gareth Stevens, New York, New York at 1-800-542-2595.

Contenido

Contents

¡Los oídos nos ayudan a escuchar!

....

Ears help us hear!

Tenemos sentidos.
El oído es uno de ellos.

....

We have senses.
Hearing is one.

Otros son la vista y el olfato.
El tacto y el gusto,
también son sentidos.

....

Others are sight and smell.
Touch and taste are
senses, too.

El oído tiene varias partes.
Algunas están dentro
de tu cabeza.

....

Ears have many parts.
Some are inside your head.

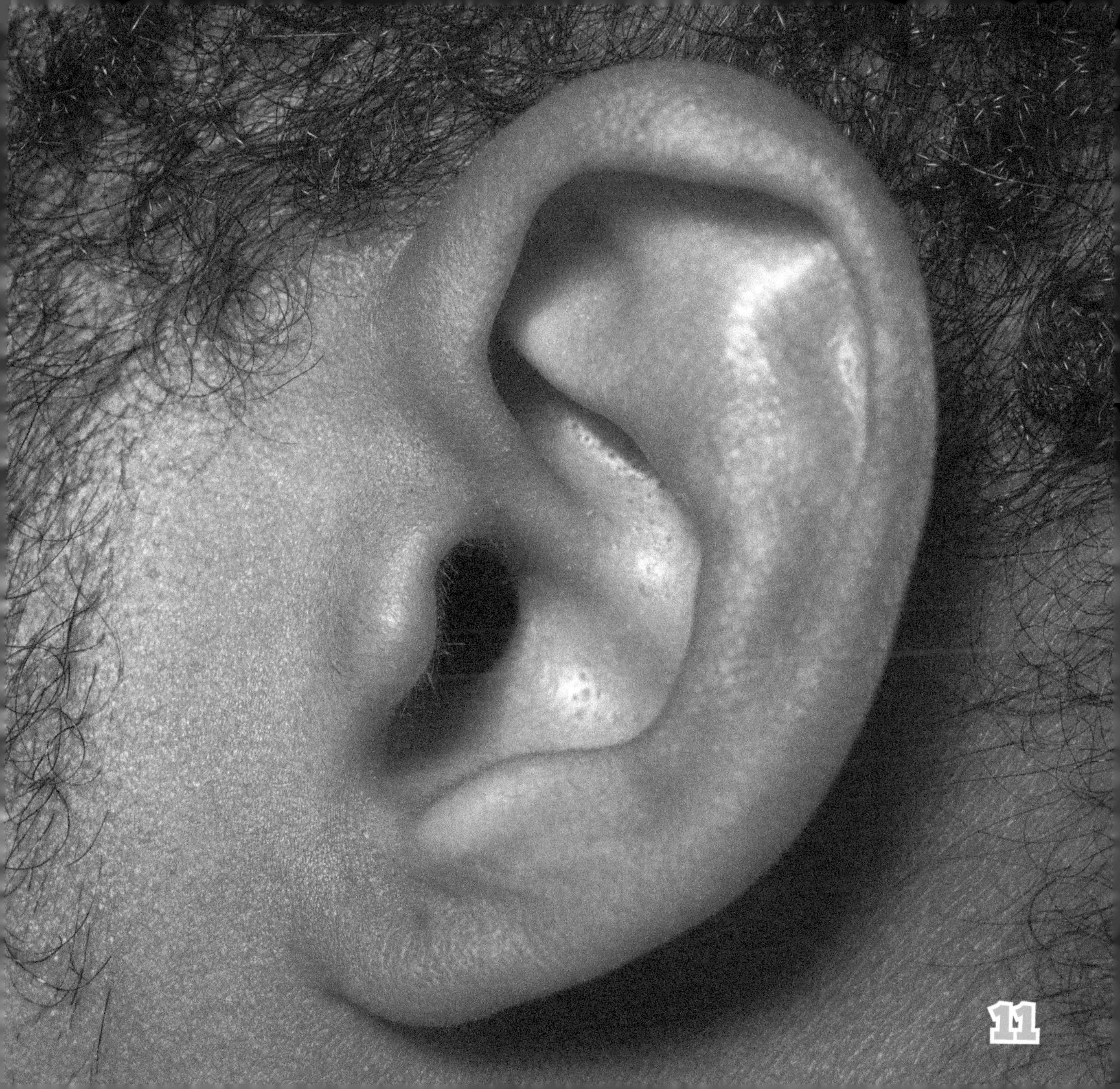

La parte que ves
es la oreja.

••••••••••••••••••••••••••••••

The part you see
is the pinna.

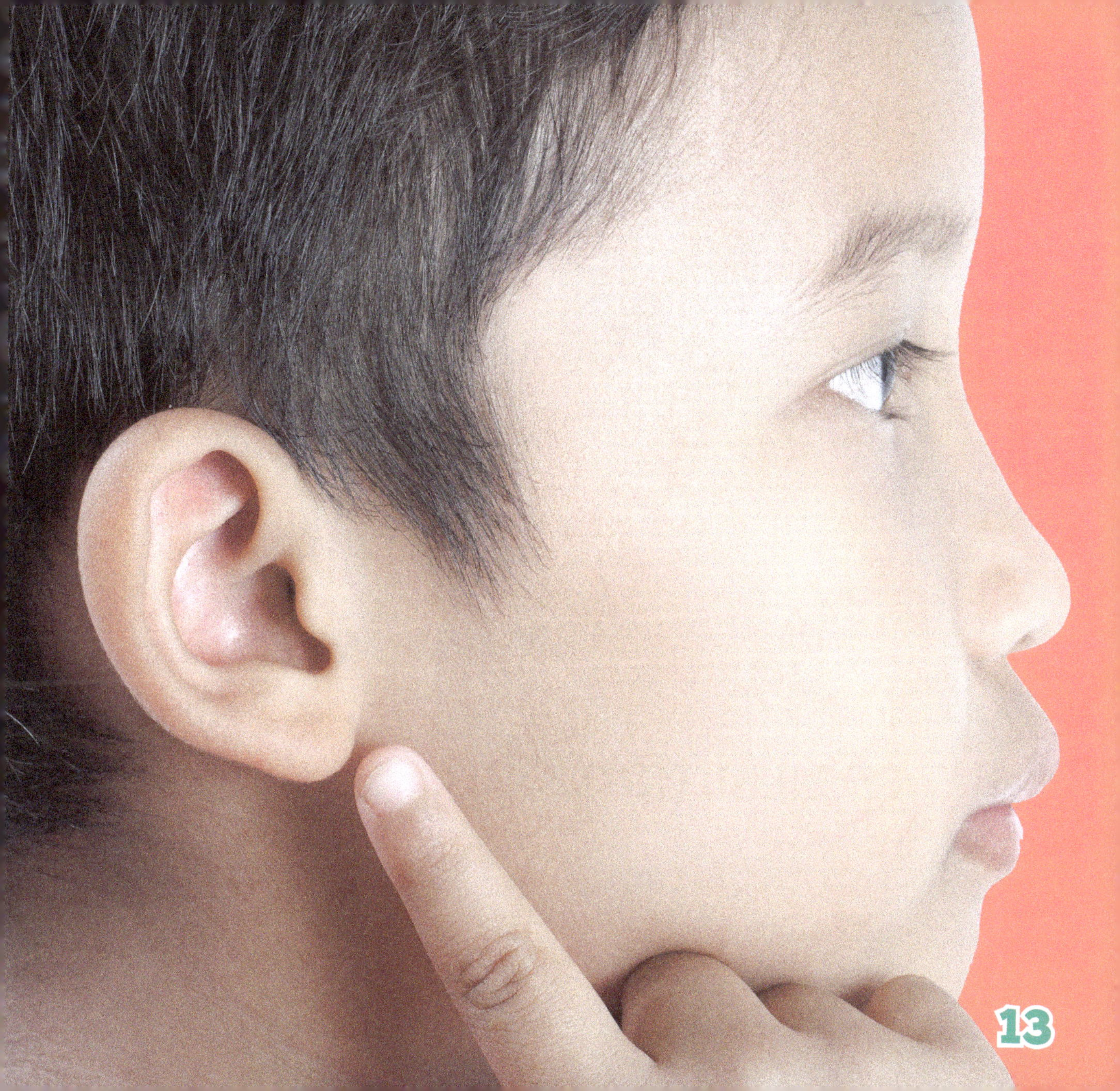

Tu oído puede dolerte.
Eso se llama dolor de oído.

••••••••••••••••••••••••••••••

Your ear may hurt.
That's an earache.

El doctor May mira mi oído.
Él es un médico de oídos.

....

Dr. May looks in my ear.
He's an ear doctor.

Los oídos te ayudan
a escuchar.
Max escucha a Jen.

....

Ears help you listen.
Max listens to Jen.

Mi perro también
tiene orejas.
Lo escucho ladrar.

....

My dog has ears, too.
I hear him bark.

¿Qué escuchas
con tus oídos?

....

What do you hear
with your ears?

Palabras que debes aprender
Words to Know

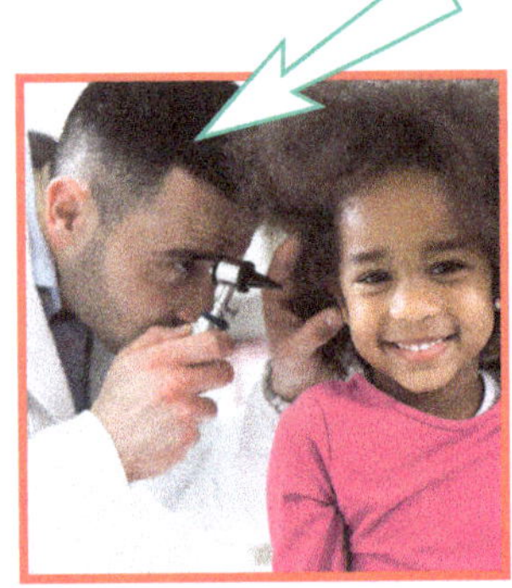
(el) doctor
doctor

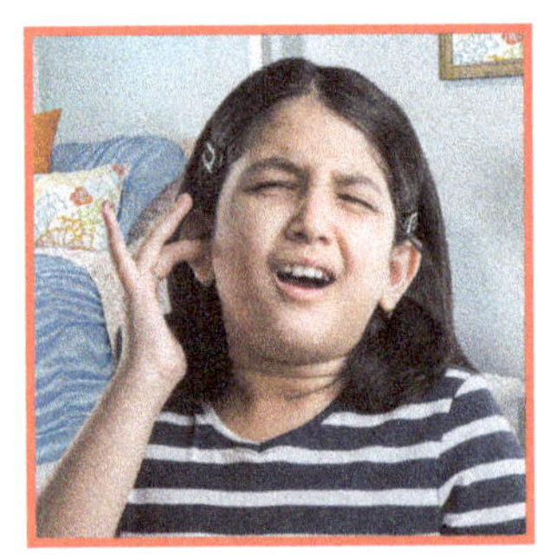
(el) dolor de oído
earache

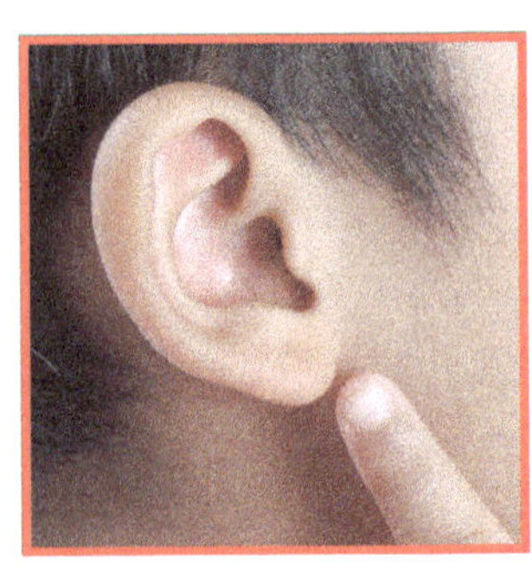
(la) oreja
pinna

Índice / Index